D0580629

Copyright © 1984 by Edward R. Emberley

Cover and title page illustrations copyright © 2005 by Edward R. Emberley

All rights reserved. In accordance with the U.S. Copyright Act of 1976, the scanning, uploading, and electronic sharing of any part of this book without the permission of the publisher is unlawful piracy and theft of the author's intellectual property. If you would like to use material from the book (other than for review purposes), prior written permission must be obtained by contacting the publisher at permissions@hbgusa.com. Thank you for your support of the author's rights.

Little, Brown and Company

Hachette Book Group

1290 Avenue of the Americas, New York, NY 10104

Visit our website at lb-kids.com

LB Kids is an imprint of Little, Brown and Company. The LB Kids name and logo are trademarks of Hachette Book Group, Inc.

The publisher is not responsible for websites (or their content) that are not owned by the publisher.

First Revised Paperback Edition: February 2006

10   9   8

Library of Congress Cataloging-in-Publication Data

Emberley, Ed.

  Ed Emberley's Picture Pie

  Summary: Shows how to cut a basic circle into arcs and curves and use the pieces to draw birds, animals, snowmen, fish, and many other objects and designs.

  1. Circle in art—Juvenile literature. 2. Drawing —Technique—Juvenile literature. [1. Circle in art. 2. Drawing—Technique] I. Title II. Title: Picture Pie.

NC825.C53E48 1984   741.2   84-9666

ISBN 978-0-316-78982-0

WKT

Printed in China

ED EMBERLEY'S

PICTURE PIE

A Cut and Paste Drawing Book

LITTLE, BROWN & COMPANY
LB kids

This book shows how a circle

divided like a pie

can be used to make pictures

of all kinds of things.

These 4 simple, basic shapes

can be put back together to make: a set of other,

more complex shapes,

(There are lots more shapes in the back of the book.)

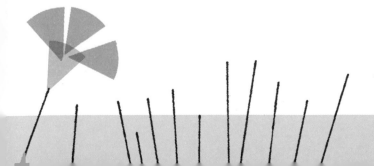

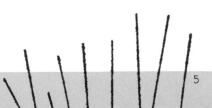

hundreds of different designs,

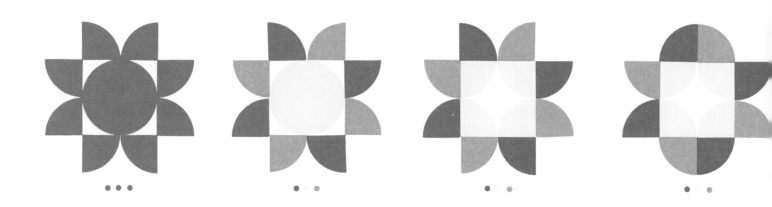

(The dots **:** show the number and color of circles used.)

  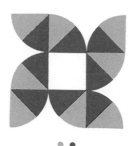 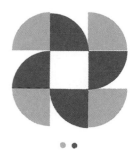

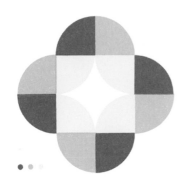 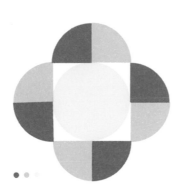  

  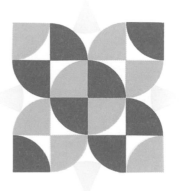

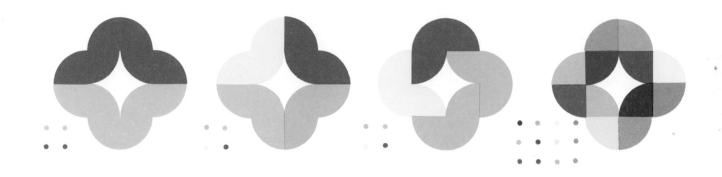

frames, borders,

and other repeat patterns,

as well as a number of birds and other things.

Here's how: (More instruction in the back of the book.)

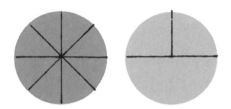

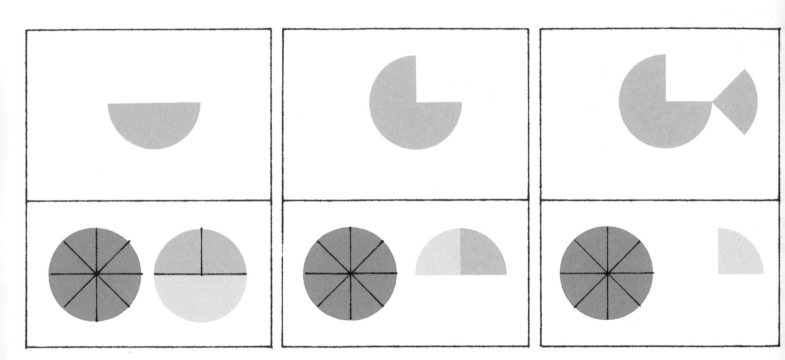

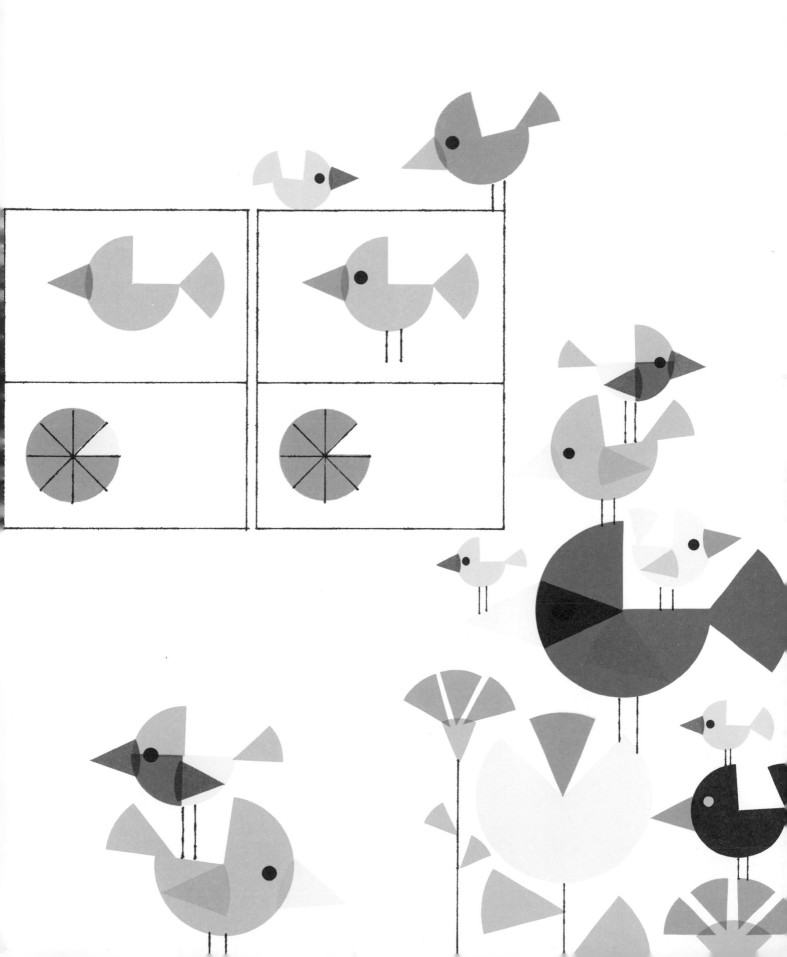

21

|| The picture pie pictures
in this book can be:

1. recreated, just for the
fun of it, as sort of
a game or puzzle

 + ▲ + •|| = ?

2. used "as is" for work
of your own

3. embellished or
modified as you
wish, or...

in cut paper for signs, posters, etc.,

A SPECIAL
INVITATION

BULLETIN
BOARD

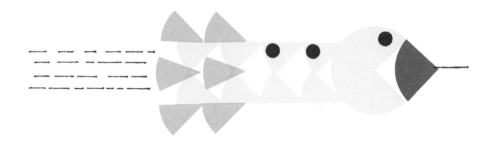

4. used as a general guide
to make something
entirely different.

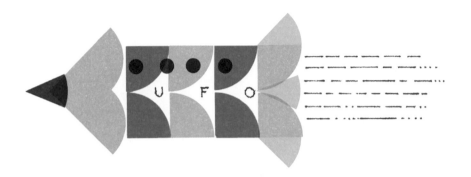

in cut wood for toys, in cut metal for jewelry,

in cut cloth for needlework, etc.

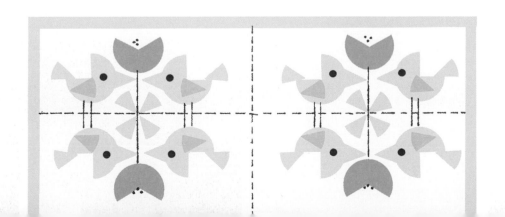

A few hints for making something

"entirely different".   You can add:

other materials,

A lot of variety can be added by
using patterned materials.

other divisions,

More variety, more possibilities.

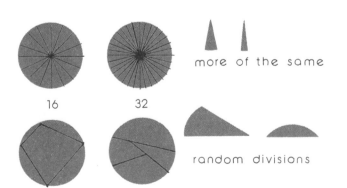

16   32   more of the same

random divisions

other circles,

By adding circles of different sizes, it is possible to make hundreds of people, animals, and other things.

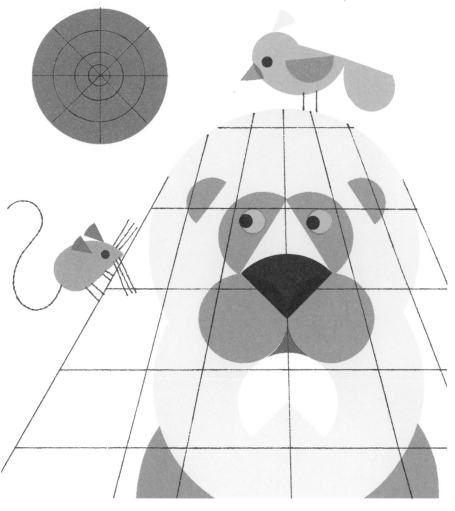

other shapes.

By adding one other shape, the square, it is possible to make thousands of people, animals, and other things.

It is possible to show only
a few of the many things
that can be made
using picture pie parts;
much has been left for
you to explore, discover,
and take pleasure in.

More Instructions:

To get started making picture pie pictures, you will need 5 things:

1. colored paper

2. something to cut it with

3. something to stick it down with

4. something to make dots and lines with

5. something to make circles with. (You can use a compass or you can draw around a cup, a can, or some other round object.)

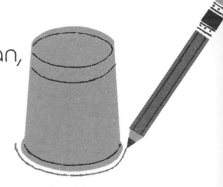

You will also have to know how to
make these 4 basic picture pie shapes.

1. start	2. fold in half	3. crease	4. unfold	5. cut along crease

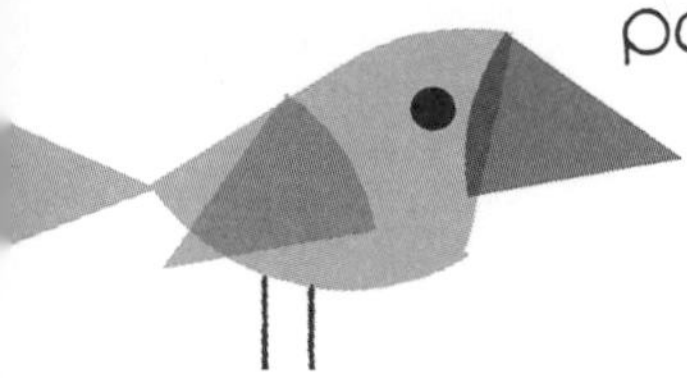

All the pictures in the first part of this book were made using these 4 basic shapes.

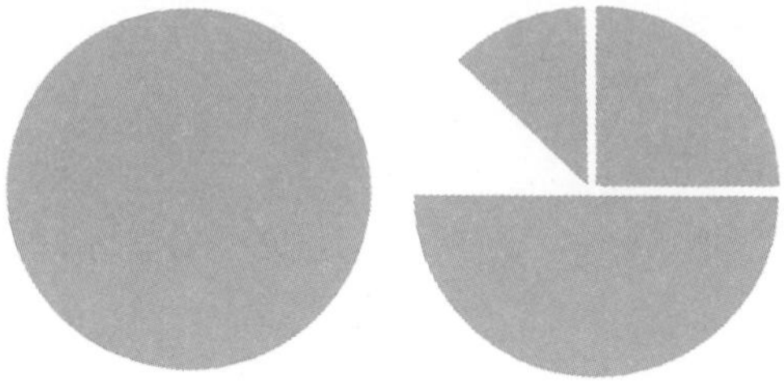

You will be able to figure out how to make many just by looking at them.

Other, more complex shapes.

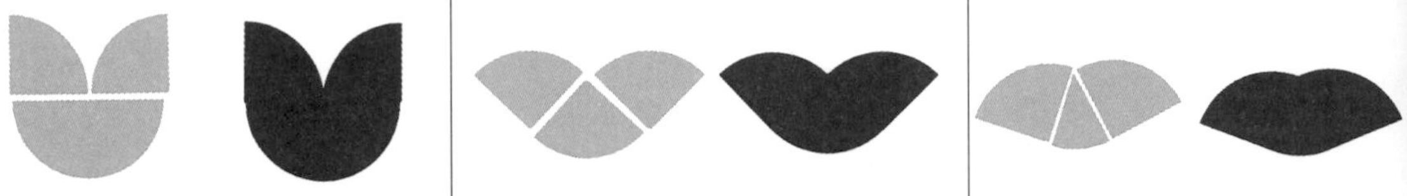

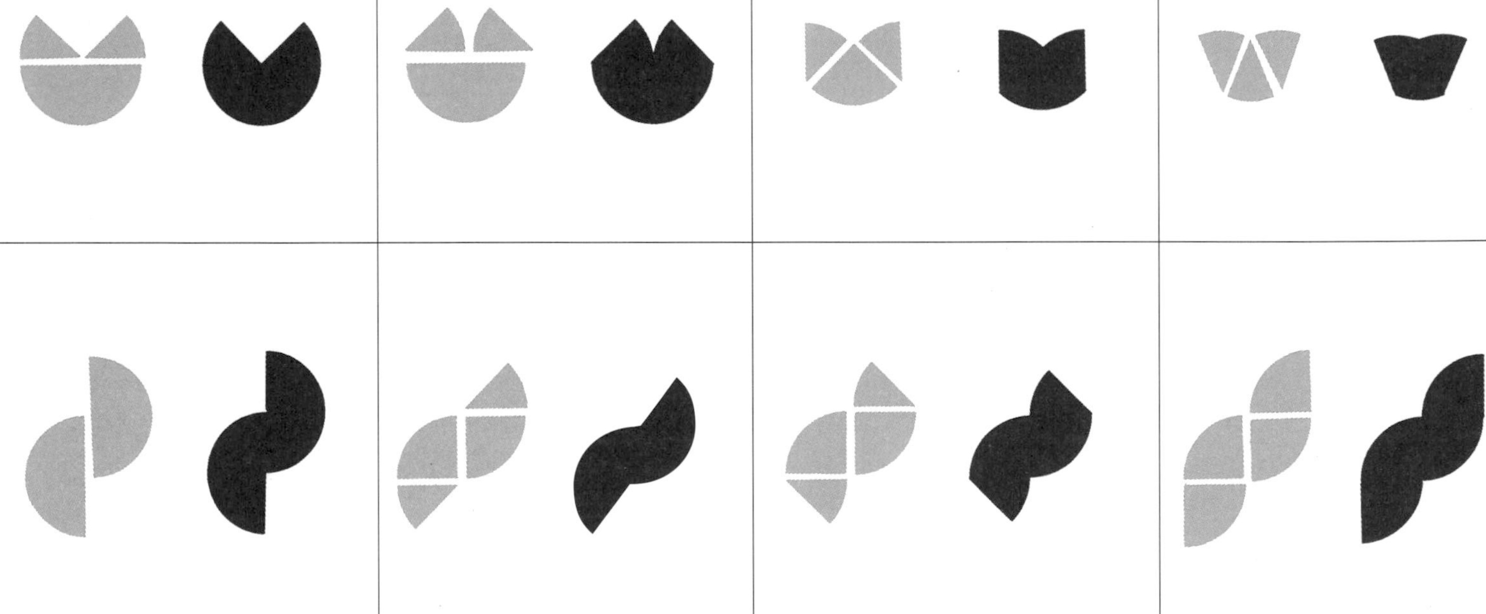

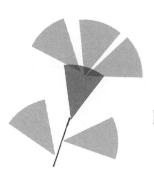

These diagrams
will help you
to figure out
how the rest
were made.

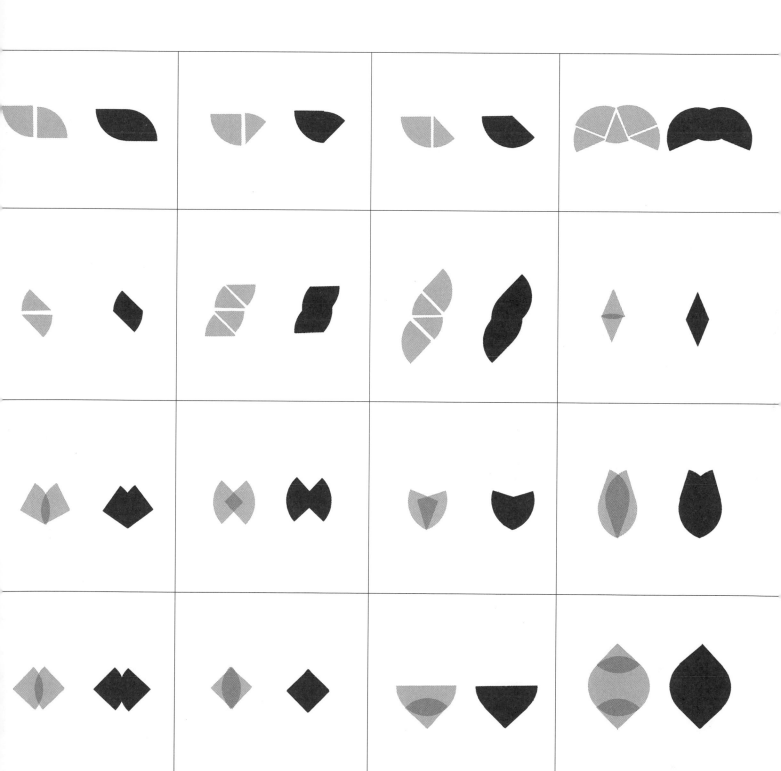

the birds

the insects

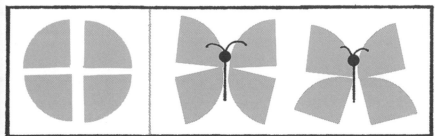

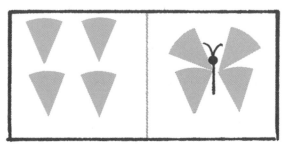

the fish

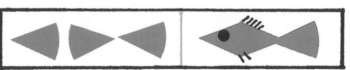

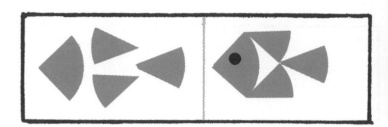

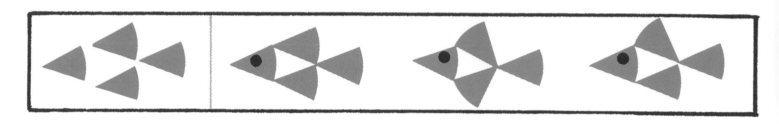

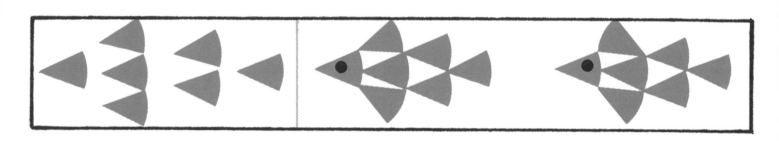

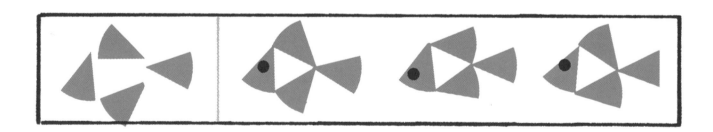

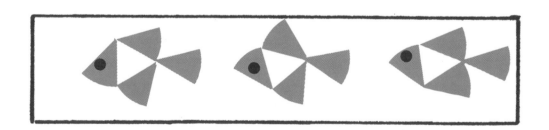

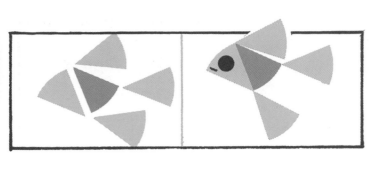

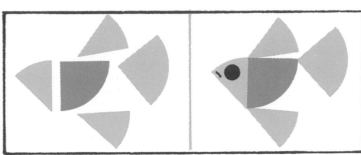

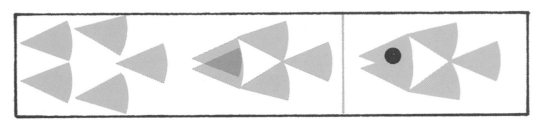

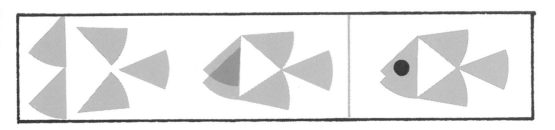

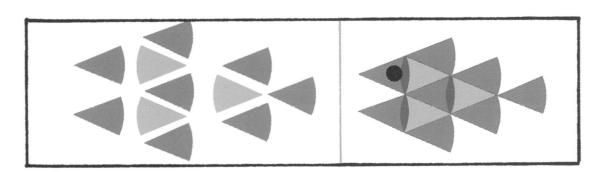

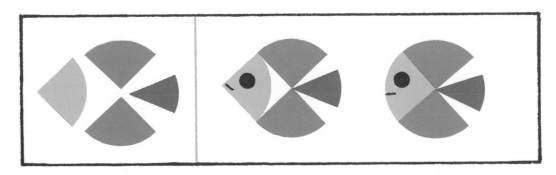

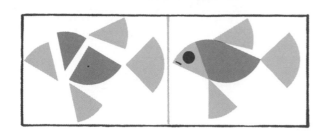

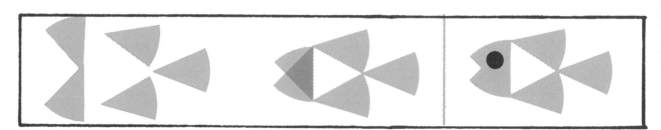

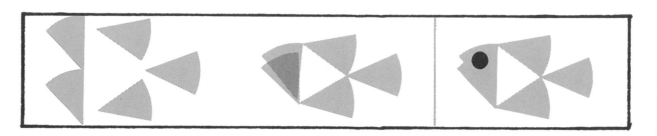

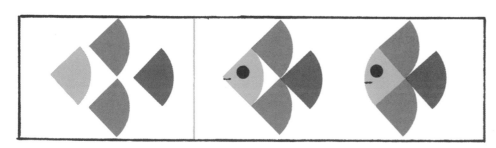

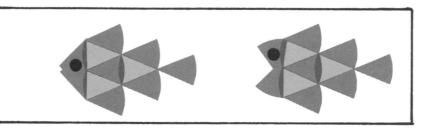

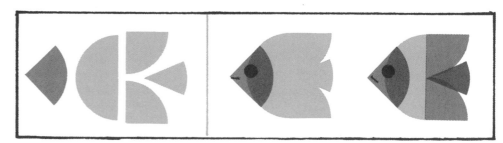

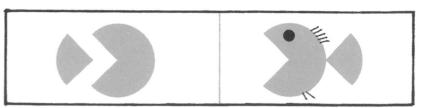

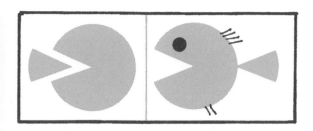

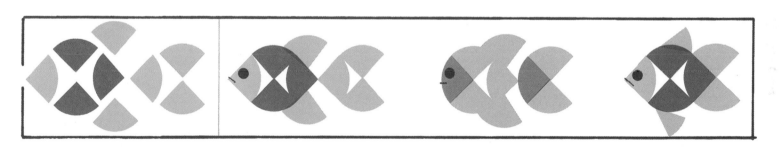

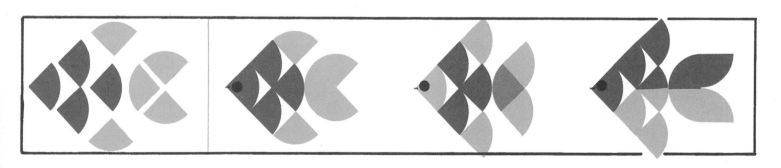

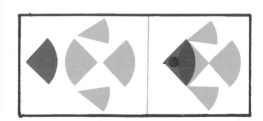

the plants

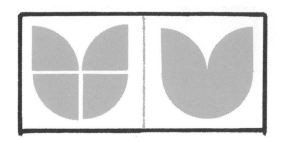

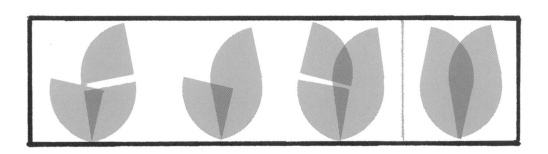

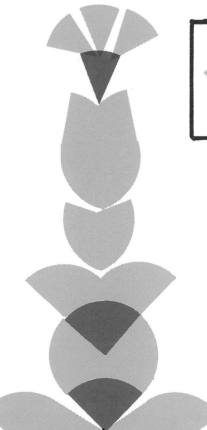

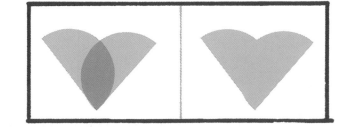

the trees

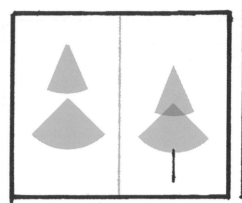

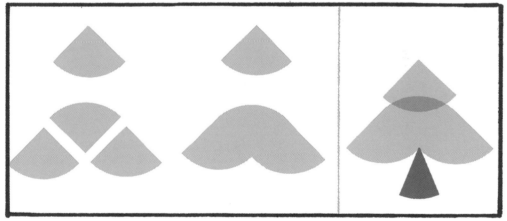
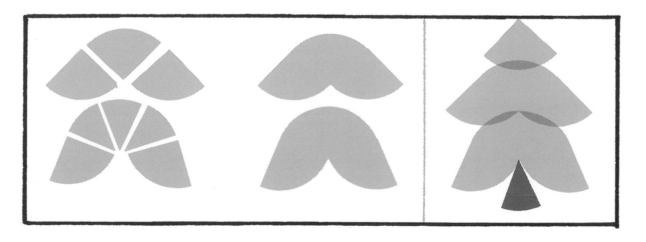

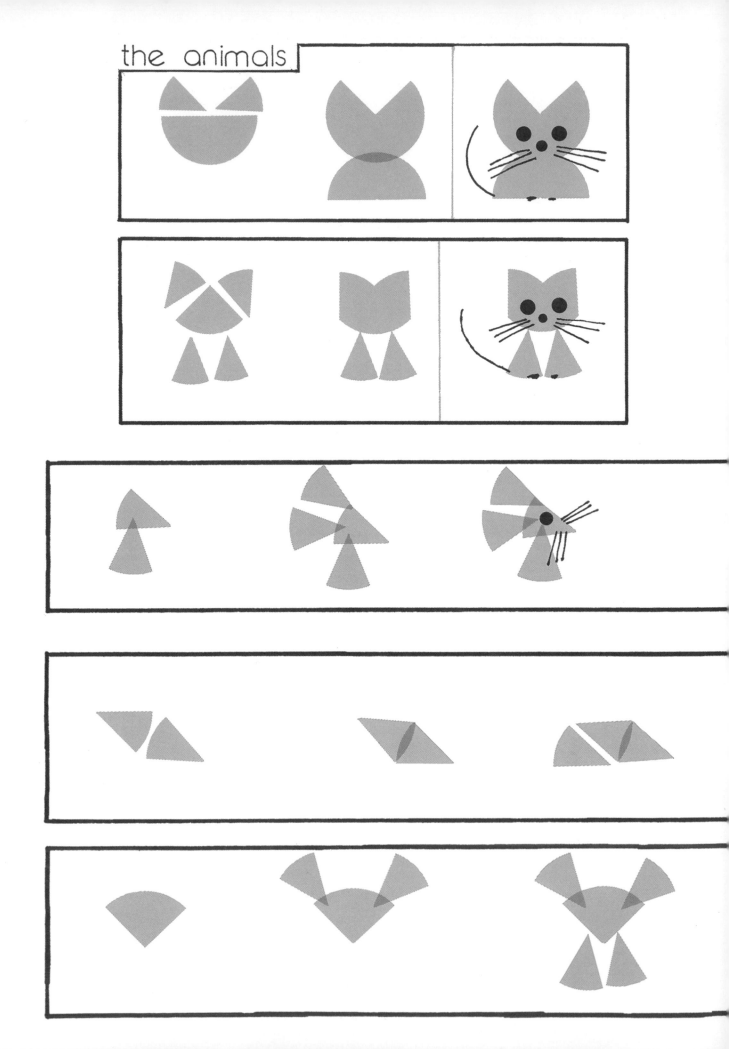

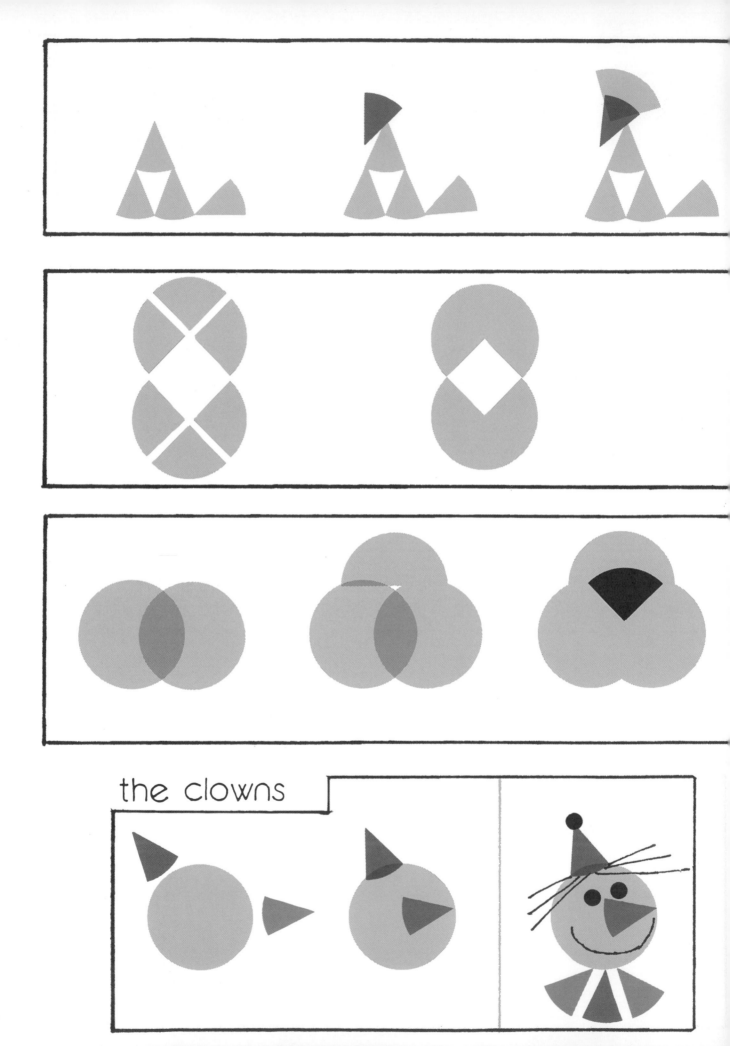

the clowns

47

three tricky ones

Ed Emberley "drew" the pictures for this book.

Barbara and Michael Emberley prepared the

300 overlays needed to print those pictures.

Rebecca Emberley "set" the type.